THE DIARY

OF

SAINT GEMMA GALGANI

ISBN–13: 978-1479239511

ISBN–10: 1479239518

This Edition: 5" x 8" Paperback CR. Also available:
Kindle Edition: ASIN: B008A7O3GM

INRI
PUBLISHERS

TABLE OF CONTENTS

PART IV
AUGUST 20TH TO SEPTEMBER 3RD 1900 29

---

[1] *Editor's Note:* Dates July 24th, August 13th and 14th 1900 have no entries by Saint Gemma Galgani.

SAINT GEMMA'S DIARY

PART I

JULY 19TH TO 23RD 1900

THURSDAY, JULY 19

This evening at last, after six days of absence of Jesus, since it was Thursday, I began my hour of prayer[2], thinking of Jesus on the Cross. Then it happened. I found myself with Him suffering and I felt a great desire to suffer and asked Jesus to give me this grace. He granted it; He approached me, took from His head the crown of thorns and placed it upon mine, and then went aside. I looked at Him silently for I was thinking; Perhaps He did not love me anymore, because He had not pressed the crown down hard upon my head as He had done at other times. Jesus understood and pressed it upon my temples. They were painful but happy moments. I then spent an hour with Jesus. I should have liked to continue with Him thus all night, but Jesus loves obedience very much; He Himself always submits to obedience, so when the hour was up He left me. Generally Jesus took the crown off when He was leaving; this time, however, He left it until about four o'clock the following afternoon.

FRIDAY, JULY 20

By four o'clock today I was tired of suffering. I presently found myself with Jesus, Who came beside me and was not sad as on the previous night; He caressed me and lifted the crown from my

---

[2] Gemma made a holy hour every Thursday evening, since her miraculous cure, something she had promised to do. She made this holy hour every Thursday until her death.

head. I then felt less pain; but when He put it upon His own head I felt no pain at all. My strength returned and I felt even better than before I began to suffer.

We talked of many things and during our conversation I asked Him not to make me confess to Father Vallini, because I did not like to. Jesus seemed disappointed, and told me that I should go at once. I promised I would. He showed His heart to me and said "I love you greatly because you are like me." "In what way, Jesus?" I asked, "because I seem so unlike you." "In accepting humiliations," He replied. Then there returned to me a vision of my past life. I saw my pride. It was always one of my greatest defects. When I was little, wherever I went I always heard it said that I was very proud. But what means Jesus has used to humiliate me, especially during this past year! At last I understand what God was doing with me. May Jesus be always thanked. Then my God added that with time He would make a saint of me. Of this last I will say no more for that is impossible to happen to me. He told me of something to say to the confessor and blessed me. I knew Jesus would be away from me for some days. But how good He is! Scarcely had He gone when my Angel Guardian appeared, who with his continual charity, vigilance, and patience assists me. Oh Jesus, I have promised always to obey you. I affirm it anew.

SATURDAY, JULY 21

My dearest Mother of Sorrows came to pay me a little visit as she is accustomed to on Saturday.

She seemed very unhappy and looked as if she had been weeping. Then she smiled, saying to me:

"Gemma, do you wish to repose on my breast?" I approached her and knelt; she raised me, kissed me on the forehead and disappeared.

This evening, after confessing to Father Vallini, I felt suddenly agitated and disturbed; it was a sign that the devil was near. Later, internally and also externally, I was all in a tempest; I should have preferred to go to bed and sleep rather than to pray, but no, I began to say three invocations, which I usually say every evening to the Sacred Heart of Mary. The enemy, who had been hidden for some hours, appeared in the form of a very small man, but so horrible that I was almost overcome with fear.

Continuing to pray, all at once I began to feel many blows on the shoulder which continued for about half an hour. Then my Angel Guardian came and asked me what the matter was; I begged him to stay with me all night, and he said to me, "But I must sleep." "No," I replied, "Angels of Jesus do not sleep." "Nevertheless," he replied, smiling, "I ought to rest. Where shall you put me?" I begged him to remain near me.

I went to bed; after that he seemed to spread his wings and come over my head. In the morning he was still there.

SUNDAY, JULY 22

The devil, in the form of a great black dog, put his paws upon my shoulders, making every bone in my body ache. At times I believed that he would mangle me; then one time, when I was taking holy water, he twisted my arm so cruelly that I fell to the earth in great pain.

After a while I remembered that I had around my neck the relic of the Holy Cross. Making the Sign of the Cross, I became calm. Jesus let me see Himself, but only for a short time, and He strengthened me anew to suffer and struggle.

At dinner time, there had come to me an evil thought which my Angel understood and he said to me; "Daughter, do you wish me to go away?" I was ashamed. These words I heard very distinctly and I did not know whether or not others also heard him.

While in church yesterday, he reprimanded me, saying: "The glory of Jesus and the place where you are, merit another kind of conduct," because at that time I had raised my eyes to look at two children, to see how they were dressed.

Last night, while in bed, He reproved me again, saying, that instead of progressing in his teachings I was becoming constantly worse and continually slackening in well–doing.

I am always conscious when these things happen to me. It seems to me that no matter what I do, I do not succeed in preparing myself for the visit of the Mother of Sorrows or Brother Gabriel[3].

MONDAY, JULY 23

I went to bed, I slept, and slept well; after a quarter of an hour, for my sleep is always brief, I saw at the foot of my bed, on the ground, that usual ominous black creature, very black, very small. I knew who it was and said, "Have you begun again the business of not letting me sleep?" "What, sleep, why don't you pray?" he replied.

"I shall pray later," I said. "Now it is time to sleep."

"For two days you have not been able to be recollected; well, let's do what I want." He began to give me blows, until he jumped up suddenly and rolled on the ground. I do not know what happened but I smiled for I did not have any fear of him today; he said, "Today I can do nothing to you but I'll take care of you another time."

I asked him: "Why can't you? If you can do it other times, why can't you now? I know – I am the same, but I have Jesus (the relic) on my neck."

Then he said to me: "What have you in this room? Take off the belt[4] (Saint Gabriel's) you wear and then we shall see."

I insisted that I had nothing but I knew what he meant. After this, I smiled at him as he stood there devoured with rage. He told me that if I prayed I would suffer all the more.

"It doesn't matter," I said, "I suffer for Jesus."

In short, today I was much entertained by him. I saw him very angry; he has sworn to make me pay for it.

He waited until this evening, but by the grace of God he was not able to remain very long; he gave me three violent blows so that afterward going to bed took much time. At certain times he ran off and with such fear that I did not know what the matter was.

I myself, was scarcely able to move.

---

[3] St. Gabriel Possenti.

[4] St. Gabriel Possenti had, recently in a vision, given Gemma his belt that the Passionists wear.

How often I called Jesus! But he did not come; I prayed that my Angel Guardian should lead me to Jesus, but everything was in vain. He said to me: "Tonight Jesus will not come to bless you nor will I."

I was frightened then because if Jesus did not bless me I could not get up .... He saw that I was about to weep and said: "But you know, Jesus will send someone. And if you knew who it was, how happy you would be."

My mind flew at once to Brother Gabriel. I asked him, but he made no reply, he kept me in suspense for some time. At last he said to me: "But if Jesus does send Brother Gabriel to bless you, what will you do? Do not speak to him if you do not want to disobey the Confessor." "No, I will not speak," I replied impatiently, "but how can Brother Gabriel bless me?" "It is Jesus who sends him; he has sent him other times to bless you. But will you manage to be silent and obey?" "Yes, yes, I will obey; let him come."

After a little while Brother Gabriel came. What a frenzy seized me then! I wanted to speak to him, but I was good and checked myself[5]. He blessed me with certain Latin words which I have remembered well, and then he suddenly departed. Oh, then I could not help saying: "Brother Gabriel, ask our Mother to bring you to me Saturday." He turned to me smiling and said:

"You are to be good," and saying this took from his waist his black belt and said "Do you want it again?" I wanted it very much indeed: "That helps me so much when you let me wear it; please give it to me now." He shook his head to indicate that he would give it to me Saturday and left me. He told me that the belt was the one which had liberated me from the devil the night before.

It happened today as usual. I had gone to bed, in fact I was asleep, but the devil did not wish this. He presented himself in a disgusting manner; he tempted me but I was strong. I commended myself to Jesus asking that He take my life rather than have me offend Him. What horrible temptations those were! All displease me but those against Holy Purity make me

---

[5] During this period, St. Gemma's confessor, Monsignor Volpi, had ordered Gemma not to speak to any of the persons in her visions, although she was allowed to speak to her Angel.

most wretched. Afterward he left me in peace and the Angel Guardian came and assured me that I had not done anything wrong. I complained somewhat, because I wished his help at such times, and he said that whether I saw him or not, he would be always above my head. Also, yesterday he promised that in the evening Jesus would come to see me.

Yesterday evening I waited with impatience for the moment to go to my room; I took the crucifix and went to bed. My Angel was willing to have me go to bed because of the order of the Confessor. I felt myself becoming recollected. Jesus came and stood by my side. What beautiful moments those were!

I asked Him if He would love me always, and He replied with these words: "My daughter, I have enriched you with so many beautiful things without any merit on your part and you ask me if I love you? I fear so much for you." "Why?" I asked. "Oh daughter, on the days when you enjoy My presence you are all fervor, it costs you no fatigue to pray. Now instead you are wearied by prayer and negligence in your duties seeks to insinuate itself in your heart. Oh daughter, why do you speak thus? Tell me, in the past, did prayer seem long as it does now? Some little penance you do, but how long you wait before resolving upon it."

Finally I commended His poor sinner to Him. He blessed me and in going away said to me: "Remember that I have created you for Heaven; you have nothing to do with the earth."

PART II

JULY 25TH TO AUGUST 4TH 1900

WEDNESDAY, JULY 25

And what about today? What shall I say today? I find no peace; pride predominates over me more than in earlier times. I suffered much to complete even a small act of humiliation. About what happened to me yesterday I shall speak very little; I do not control my tongue and for this reason I cause other people to suffer.

For obedience to my confessor I must speak very little and never with people who know about my experiences. A few days ago when Father Norberto came, I hid instantly; another time he came and I did the same; I was ready, truth be said, to be obedient, but then what happened to me? After a few days I chanced to be speaking to another friar about this and I invented a big lie, saying that it was Mrs. Cecilia who had made me hide; but that was not true, it was I who did it on my own.

I don't know how Father Norberto came to learn of this, but instantly he referred the matter to Mrs. Cecilia, who was very hurt. But I was no less hurt. She interrogated me about whether I had really spoken and I answered no, because I had completely forgotten about it; but there's always the one who makes me remember everything; my guardian Angel came and reproached me, saying: "Gemma, what's this, even lying? Don't you remember a few days ago, when as punishment for telling Brother Famiano about your experiences, I made you stay half an hour ... ?"

I then recalled everything well (I must say that my guardian angel, every time I do a bad thing, punishes me; not an evening passes that I do not have some punishment) and he commanded me to go to Mrs. Cecilia and tell everything and beg her in his name to forgive me.

I promised to do this, sure! The day passed, then came the evening and I never made that little act of humility. My angel reminded me again, saying that if I didn't go to her and tell her everything, that night the devil would come.

Well, that threat I could not ignore, and so I went to her room. She was in bed and the lamp was out; I couldn't believe it: this way she would not see me. As well as I could I told her everything, but in a forced way; it was a great shame, my being unable to humiliate myself. Finally, after she said all would be forgotten, I went to my room. Yes, of course! She said all was forgotten but it was impossible. I asked Jesus many times for forgiveness and also my beloved Angel, and I went to bed. What a horrible night! My Angel, because of the great resistance I had put up before accepting my humiliation left me alone, and with a few visits by the enemy. I could not sleep because my conscience was ill at ease; how I was troubled!

THURSDAY, JULY 26

In the morning my guardian Angel finally came and he reproached me harshly, very harshly and left me once again alone and afflicted. I received Communion but, my God, in what a state! Jesus did not make himself felt. When after all this I was able to be alone, then I let out my feelings freely; I was at fault, I realize that; but if I can say one thing, I did not wish to cause certain displeasures to certain persons, but my evil inclinations are so bad that I often fall into these things. For more than an hour Jesus made me stay in that state; I cried and I was afflicted. Then Jesus had pity on me and he came; He caressed me and made me promise not to do these things again, and He blessed me.

I have to say that in what happened yesterday I told three lies, I had angry thoughts, and I had the idea of avenging myself against whoever had tattled on me, but Jesus prohibited me from speaking with Brother Famiano and with others. I quickly became calm, and to be even more so, I ran to confession.

Then in the evening, after saying my prayers, I set out to do the usual Holy Hour prayer. Jesus stayed with me throughout; I was in bed[6], as usual, because otherwise I would not have been able to remain with my beloved Jesus and suffer with him. I suffered a lot; He proved anew his love toward me by giving me His crown of thorns until the following day; Jesus loves me most on Friday. That evening He took back the crown, saying He was happy with me and as He caressed me He said: "Daughter, if I add other crosses, do not be afflicted." I promised, and He left me.

FRIDAY, JULY 27

This Friday I suffered even more, because I had to do some chores and at every moment I thought I would die. Indeed, my aunt had commanded me to fetch water: I felt so exhausted I thought the thorns went into my brain (but this was all my imagination), and a drop of blood began to appear at my temple. I hurriedly cleaned up so she barely noticed it. She asked me if maybe I had fallen and cut my head; I told her that I had scratched myself with the chain from the well. Then I went to the nuns, it was 10:00am and I stayed with them until about 5:00pm. Then I returned home, but Jesus already had removed the crown.

SATURDAY, JULY 28

The night passed very well; in the morning my guardian angel came: he was happy and he told me to take a piece of paper and write what he would dictate:

Here it is:

"Remember, my daughter, that whoever truly loves Jesus speaks little and bears everything. I order you, on behalf of Jesus, not to give your opinion unless you are asked; never to hold to your own wishes, but to submit immediately. Obey promptly your confessor and others he designates, without answering back; when it is necessary, make only one reply, and be sincere with your confessor and with others. When you have committed some

---

[6] During this period, Gemma's confessor Monsignor Volpi, had ordered Gemma to go to bed in the evening, and not linger in her room in prayer.

fault of omission, accuse yourself instantly, without waiting to be asked.

Finally, remember to guard your eyes, and think, eyes that have been mortified will see the beauty of Heaven."

After saying these things he blessed me and said I should go to communion. I went right away; it was the first time in nearly a month that Jesus had made himself felt.

I told him all of what was happening and he kept me with him a long while, because I received communion at 8:30am and when I returned to my senses it was much later. I ran home and on the way the clock struck 10:15am. I was good and found myself in the same position that I had been in during communion, and as I got up I saw that my guardian angel was above my head with his wings spread. He accompanied me home himself and warned me not to pray during the day, not until nightfall, because I could not be safe. In fact I realized that I was safe from the others in the household, but not from my sister, because she had stuffed the keyhole and it was impossible to lock myself in; then my aunts intervened and in the evening I could close the door.

Toward evening, I went to the Fifteen Saturdays at St. Maria Bianca;[7] the Blessed Virgin told me She would not be paying me her usual little visit because in the past few days I had disgusted Jesus. I said to Her that Jesus had forgiven me, but She said: "I don't forgive my daughters so easily; I absolutely want you to become perfect: we'll see if Saturday I can come and bring Brother Gabriel." Nevertheless, She blessed me and I resigned myself.

But I do not lack for temptation; one, a strong one, was Saturday evening: the devil came and said to me: "Good, good girl! Sure, go and write everything: don't you know that everything you write is my work and if you are discovered, think about the scandal! Where will you go to hide? I pass you off as a saint, but you are deluded."

I felt so badly that out of desperation I swore that when Mrs. Cecilia returned I would destroy what I had written. In the

---

[7] The parish church of the Giannini family.

meantime I tried to tear this writing up but I couldn't; I didn't have the strength, or else I just don't know what happened.

SUNDAY, JULY 29

I remained in this state until yesterday morning, Sunday, without being able to collect myself; my guardian Angel, however, does not leave me: he gives me strength, and I must say that Sunday I had no appetite but he himself ordered me to eat, as he did today also. Every evening he did not fail to bless me, but also to punish me and yell at me.

Today, Sunday, I feel a great need for Jesus but it is already late and I no longer have any hope; I expect to spend the night free and alone.

But Jesus came, you know! How He reproached me because I had not gone to Communion. This is how Jesus reproached me: "Why, oh daughter, am I so often deprived of your visits? You know how much I yearn for you to come to me when you are good."

I fell on my knees in front of Jesus and in tears I said: "But how can this be, my Jesus, aren't you tired of putting up with me and all my coldness?"

"Daughter," he answered," see to it that from now on not a day goes by without your coming to me, try to keep your heart pure and adorned with every possible care. Drive all self–love away from your heart and anything else that is not entirely mine, and then come to me without fear."

He blessed me, along with all the members of the Sacro Collegio; and went away; indeed, in the end he advised me to have a little more strength in combating the enemy, telling me to take no account of those words because the devil is always a liar who seeks every means to make me fall, especially about obedience. "Obey, my daughter," he repeated, "obey instantly and cheerfully, and to achieve victory in this beautiful virtue, pray to my Mother who loves you so much." I would have wanted to tell him that yesterday his Mother didn't wish to come, but He disappeared.

MONDAY, JULY 30

This morning I went to communion. I did not want to: I was not at peace with my conscience; I lingered until 9:00am, thinking if I should go or not; then Jesus won and I went to Communion, but how? With what coldness! I was completely unable to feel Jesus.

Today I was not able to collect myself at all; I was bad, I got angry, but only by myself, no one else saw me: I cried so, so much, because my sister Angelina did not want to leave my room. Yesterday evening, Sunday, for spite, she stayed in my room until 11:00pm, making fun of me, saying that she wanted to see me go in ecstasy; today again the same thing. She wrote a letter yesterday to Bagni di S. Giuliano and spoke a lot about me and my experiences. These things, which I should be accepting happily and with thanks to Jesus, instead upset me, and I almost have moments of despair.

While I was in that state, my guardian angel who was watching me, said:

"Why are you so upset, my daughter? You have to suffer something, you know, for Jesus." (In truth, what displeased me most were certain words that my sister had said out loud to me), and to this my angel responded: "You are worthy only to be scorned because you have offended Jesus."

Then he calmed me, sat at my side, and said gently, very gently: "Oh daughter, don't you know that you must conform in every way to the life of Jesus? He suffered so much for you, don't you know that you must on every occasion suffer for him? Furthermore, why do you give this displeasure to Jesus, of neglecting to meditate on his Passion every day?" It was true: I recalled that I did a meditation on the Passion only on Fridays and Thursdays. "You must do it every day, remember that." Finally he said to me: "Be brave, be brave! This world is not a place for rest: rest will come after death; for now you must suffer, and suffer all things, to save some soul from eternal death." I begged him urgently to ask my Mother to come to me a little, because I had so many things to tell Her, and he said yes. But this evening She did not come.

TUESDAY, JULY 31

We are at Tuesday; I run to Communion but in what a state! I promised Jesus to be good and to change my life; I said it, but He didn't answer anything; I also asked that He send his Mother, and also mine, and he responded: "Are you worthy?" I was ashamed, and I said nothing more. Then he added: "Be good and soon She will come with Brother Gabriel."

It's been since Sunday that I have been unable to collect myself; nonetheless I thanked Jesus. When my guardian angel comes, I am awake, and my head does not take off; Jesus, my Mom and sometimes Brother Gabriel make my head take off; but I always stay where I am; I always find myself in the same place, it's just that my head departs. What a great need I have for my Mother! If Jesus would grant me this, afterward I would be better. How am I supposed to go so long without Mom?

WEDNESDAY AND THURSDAY, AUGUST 1 AND 2

Wednesday, I could not collect myself at all. Nor Thursday; from time to time my guardian angel would say something to me, but I was always awake; in fact, Wednesday evening, interiorly I thought I might be deceived by the devil; my guardian angel calmed me by saying: "Obedience."

Now coming to Thursday. As usual out of obedience I went to bed; I began my prayers and immediately collected myself. For a while I had been feeling ill. I stayed all alone; when I was suffering Jesus wasn't there and I suffered only in my head. My confessor asked me this morning if I had had the signs, and I said no. They hurt a lot but not compared to my head.

Poor Jesus! He made me stay alone for about an hour but then He came and showed up like this, all bloodied, saying: "I am the Jesus of Father Germano." I did not believe him, and you know why.[8] I am always fearful, always. I pronounced these words: "Long live Jesus and Mary" and then I understood. He gave me a bit of strength but internally I was still afraid, and he

---

[8] Gemma is referring the the Devil.

said: "Do not fear: I am the Jesus of Father Germano."[9] He urged me of His own free will, without my even suggesting it, to pray for Mother Maria Teresa of the Infant Jesus because she is in Purgatory and suffering greatly. Jesus wants her quickly with him, I think.

FRIDAY, AUGUST 3

Today I slept a little, then I felt completely collected; after becoming collected I felt my head take off: I was with Jesus. How happy I was! Yes, I suffered so much in my head; I complained a little because He is leaving me alone. I begged Him also to tell me when Mother Maria Teresa would be in Heaven. He said: "Not yet; she's still suffering." I commended my poor sinner to Him and He blessed me and all the members of the Sacro Collegio and He left me in a happy state.

This evening I felt I could not collect myself; I said a few evening prayers and went to bed. To tell the truth, I foresaw a bit of a storm because Jesus had warned me a few days ago, saying: "The enemy will try you with one final battle, but it will be the last because now that is enough." I could not help but thank Him for the strength He had always given me, and I prayed that He would want to give me strength for this final test as well, that is to say last night.

I went to bed, as you know well, with the intention of sleeping; slumber was not long in coming when almost instantly a tiny, tiny man appeared, all covered in black hair. What a fright! He put his hands on my bed and I thought he wanted to hit me: "No, no," he said, "I am not able to hit you, don't be afraid," and as he said this he lay down on the bed.

I called Jesus to help me but he did not come, but this doesn't mean he abandoned me. As soon as I called his name I felt liberated, but it was sudden.

Other times I had called Jesus but He had never been ready like last night.

---

[9] Gemma had not yet met Father Germano, although Jesus had shown him to her in a vision and told her that he would someday be her spiritual director.

You should have seen the demon afterward, how angry! He rolled around on the floor, cursing; he made one last effort to take away the cross I had with me but then he instantly fell backward.

How good Jesus was with me last night. The devil, after that last effort, turned toward me and said that since he had not been able to do anything, he wished to torment me the rest of the night. "No," I told him; I called my guardian angel, who opened his wings and alighted next to me; he blessed me and the bad devil ran away. Jesus be thanked.

This morning I learned that at the very moment the devil was rising in fury, the scapular of Our Lady of Sorrows had been placed on me[10] and I realized that when the devil was trying to take something off of me, it could be nothing but that. My Mother, Our Lady of Sorrows, also be thanked.

SATURDAY, AUGUST 4

Here I am at Saturday: it's the day destined for me to see my Mom, but should I hope for it?

Finally evening has arrived. I set out to recite the Sorrowful Mysteries of the Rosary; at first I abandoned myself, that is to say, I placed myself in God's will, to spend that Saturday also without seeing Our Lady of Sorrows; but for Jesus this offering was enough of a sacrifice and he fulfilled my wishes. At some point, I'm not sure where in the rosary, I felt completely collected and with this collection, as usual, quickly my head took off, and without realizing it, I found myself (it seemed to me) in front of Our Lady of Sorrows.

Upon first seeing her, I was a little afraid; I did all I could to assure myself that it was truly Jesus' Mother and She gave me every sign to assure me. After a few moments I felt entirely happy but I was so moved by seeing myself, so little compared to her, and so content, that I could not say a word except to repeat the name "Mom".

---

[10] By Ce-cilia Giannini.

She stared, really stared, at me, laughing, and approached to caress me, and She said I should calm down. Yes, of course, happiness and emotion grew in me, and She, maybe fearing that it would be bad for me (as happened other times, indeed one time, which I did not tell about, when for the great consolation I felt in seeing Jesus again, my heart started beating with such force that I was obliged, on the orders of my confessor, to tie a tight, tight bandage around that point) left me, saying that I should go and rest. I obeyed promptly, and in one second I was in bed and She did not delay her coming; then I was calm.

I also must say that upon first seeing these things, these figures (that certainly could have been deceptions), I am initially taken with fear; then fear is followed quickly by joy. However that may be, this is what happens to me. I spoke with Her about some of my desires, the most important one being that she should bring me with her to Heaven; this I said to her several times. She answered: "Daughter, you must suffer still more."

"I will suffer up there," I wanted to say, "in Heaven."

"Oh no," was her reply, "in Heaven there is no more suffering; but I will bring you there very soon," She said.

She was near my bed, so beautiful, I contemplated her and could not get enough. I commended my sinner to her; She smiled: that was a good sign ... I further commended to her various persons who were dear to me, in particular those to whom I have a big debt of gratitude. And this I had to do also on the order of my confessor, who last time beseeched me to commend them fervently to Our Lady of Sorrows, saying that I could do nothing for them but that the Blessed Virgin may ask on my behalf and bestow on them every grace.

I feared that She would leave me at any moment and so I called her repeatedly and said She should take me with her. Her presence made me forget about my protector, Brother Gabriel. I asked about him, why hadn't She brought him along, and She said: "Because Brother Gabriel demands more exact obedience from you." She had something to tell me for Father Germano; to these last words She did not answer.

While we were talking together She constantly held my hand, and then She let go; I did not want her to go and I was about to cry; then She said:

"My daughter, that's enough; Jesus wants this sacrifice from you, now it's time for Me to leave you." Her words calmed me and I answered with tranquility: "So be it, the sacrifice is done." She left. Who could describe precisely how beautiful, how beloved is the Heavenly Mother? No, for certain there is no comparison. When will I have the good fortune of seeing Her again?

PART III

AUGUST 5TH TO 19TH 1900

SUNDAY, AUGUST 5

Today, Sunday, I prayed to my guardian Angel to grant me the favor of going to tell Jesus that I would not be able to do a meditation because I did not feel well; I would do it that evening. But that evening I had no desire; I went to bed and made preparations for meditation but collected myself only internally. My head did not take off; I stayed this way for an hour. Indeed, I should add that the Sunday meditation is always on the Resurrection, actually on Heaven; but Jesus makes it clearly known to me that he does not wish me to do that meditation just yet, because my mind immediately rushes to some principal point in his Passion. Let his will be done.

MONDAY, AUGUST 6

Here I am at August 6th. The days pass and here I am always in the same worldly abyss.

This evening my guardian Angel, while I was saying evening prayers, approached me and tapping me on the shoulder he said: "Gemma, why such disinclination for prayer? This distresses Jesus." "No," I answered, "it's not disinclination: but for two days I have not been feeling well." He responded:

"Do your duty with diligence and you shall see that Jesus will love you even more." For a moment he was silent and then he asked: "And Brother Gabriel?" "I don't know." "How long is it that you haven't seen him?",[11] "A long, long, long while." "Then tonight Jesus will send him." "Really? Tonight no, I would be disobeying: at night my confessor is opposed." Oh with how

---

[11] St. Gabriel Possenti CP.

much desire I would have wanted him! but I also wanted to obey. I prayed to send him in the daytime and soon, so that I could write that letter to Father Germano. I urged my guardian angel to go to Jesus and ask permission to spend the night together with me. He immediately disappeared.

I had finished prayers: I went to bed. When he had gotten permission from Jesus to come, he returned; he asked me: "How long has it been since you last prayed for the souls in Purgatory? Oh my daughter, you think of them so little! Mother Maria Teresa is still suffering, you know?" It was since morning that I had not prayed for them. He said he would like me to dedicate every little pain I suffered to the souls in Purgatory. "Every little penance gives them relief; even yesterday and today, if you had offered a little for them." I answered with a bit of astonishment: "My body was hurting; and do bodily pains relieve the souls in Purgatory?" "Yes," he said, "yes, daughter: even the smallest suffering gives relief." So I promised that from that moment onward I would offer everything for them. He added: "How much those souls suffer! Would you like to do something for them tonight? Do you want to suffer?" "Doing what?" I said. "Is it the same suffering Jesus did on Good Friday?" "No," he answered, "these are not Jesus' pains, yours will be bodily pains." I said no, because except for Thursday and Friday Jesus does not want this; the other nights He wants me to sleep. But since the souls in Purgatory, and in particular Mother Maria Teresa, are so dear to my heart, I told him I would gladly suffer for an hour.

These words satisfied him, but he saw clearly that in doing so I would have been disobedient, so he let me sleep.

This morning, when I awoke, he was still beside me; he blessed me and went away.

TUESDAY, AUGUST 7

During the day yesterday my guardian Angel promised me that in the evening I would be able to speak with Brother Gabriel. The long-awaited evening arrived; in the beginning I was sleepy, then an agitation came over me, enough to frighten me. But since Jesus was about to grant me this consolation, either before or after the consolation, He gives me some suffering. Jesus be always blessed.

Still, in undergoing this agitation I saw no one, I mean the devil; it's just that I felt very ill, but it lasted only a short while. Quickly I calmed down; suddenly I felt completely collected and then almost immediately it happened like usual; my head took off and I found myself with Brother Gabriel. What a consolation that was! For obedience I was not allowed to kiss his vestment and I restrained myself.[12] The first thing I did was ask him why he had stayed so long without visiting me. He answered that it was my fault. Of this I was sure because I am very bad.

How many beautiful things he told me about the convent and he said them with such force that it seemed to me his eyes sparkled. On his own, without my asking: "Daughter, within a few months, amidst the exultation of almost all Catholics, the new convent will be founded." "What do you mean, in a few months?" I said, "if there are still 13 months to go." "That's a few," he responded. Then, smiling, he turned to one side and knelt, clasped his hands and said: "Blessed Virgin, look: here on earth is the competition for propagating the new institute; come on, I beg you, make the abundance of celestial gifts and favors shower on all those who take part. Increase their strength, increase their zeal. It will be entirely your gift, oh Blessed Virgin."

He talked as if Our Lady of Sorrows were next to him; I could see nothing, but with such force, with such expression did he say those words that I remained amazed; it seemed like his head also had taken off.

Now I should speak about Father Germano, but my confessor said no, because ...

I also spoke of my poor sinner; he smiled, always a good sign. Finally he left me, filled with consolation.[13]

---

[12] This meant obedience to her Confessor who at that time ordered her not to touch any of the heavenly visitors.

[13] Gemma was always beseeching her heavenly visitors for the conversion of some soul or another. She called them "my poor sinners"

WEDNESDAY, AUGUST 8

Now we come to this morning. A little while after leaving the confessional, a thought came to me; thinking to myself that my confessor made too little of my sins, I was disturbed. To calm me down, my guardian Angel approached; I was in church and he pronounced these words out loud: "But tell me, who do you want to believe, your confessor or your head? Your confessor, who has continuous light and assistance, who is highly capable, or else yourself, who has nothing, nothing, nothing of all this? Oh what pride!" he said, "you want to become the teacher, guide, and director of your confessor!" I did not think further; I made an Act of Contrition and then went to Holy Communion.

THURSDAY, AUGUST 9

Today also, after having sustained with the help of God a battle with the enemy, a very strong one, my guardian Angel came reproaching me, and with great severity said: "Daughter, remember that in failing in any obedience, you always commit a sin. Why are you so reluctant in obeying your confessor? Remember also, there is no shorter or truer path than the one of obedience."

So why all this today? It was my fault. I would deserve even worse, but Jesus always shows me mercy.

Alas, what disgust I experience this evening! Since early morning I have felt so tired, but it's all laziness, bad will; still I want to overcome it, with the help of God.

It is Thursday and therefore I feel very strange; on Thursday evenings I always feel this way. Yes, suffer, suffer for sinners, and particularly for the poor souls in Purgatory, and in particular for ... And I know well why this laziness so early in the day. The other evenings it came upon me a few hours later. It was because today my guardian Angel told me that tonight Jesus wanted me to suffer a few extra hours, precisely two hours: at 9:00pm it would begin, for the souls in Purgatory, and without my confessor's permission; but usually he does not yell at me, indeed he wishes it, and I am free to do it.

Last night, around 9:00pm, I began to feel a little ill; I was quick to bed but I had been suffering already for a while: my head ached beyond measure and any movement I made caused me terrible distress. I suffered for two hours, as Jesus wished, for Mother Maria Teresa; then with great pain I undressed and got into bed and began to pray. It was very painful but in Jesus' company one would do anything!

FRIDAY, AUGUST 10

My guardian Angel said the previous evening that I was allowed to keep the thorns in my head until 5 : 00 in the afternoon on Friday; it was true, because around that time I began to collect myself completely; I hid myself in the Franciscan church and there Jesus came to me again to remove them; I was alone the whole time. How he showed me that he loved me! He encouraged me anew to suffer and he left me in a sea of consolation.

But I must say that many times, in particular on Thursday evenings, I am overcome with such sadness at the thought of having committed so many sins, they all come back to me: I am ashamed of myself, and I feel afflicted, so afflicted. Even last night, a few hours earlier, this shame came over me, this grief, and I find a little peace only in that bit of suffering Jesus sends me, offering it first for sinners, and in particular for me, and then for the souls in Purgatory.

How many consolations Jesus gives me! In how many ways he shows me his love! They are all things of my head; but if I obey, Jesus will not permit me to be deceived. Thursday evening He promised that in these days when Mrs. Cecilia was away, He would not leave me without my guardian Angel. He gave me the Angel last night and from then on he has not left me for even a moment.

This I have observed many times, and I have not spoken of it even with my confessor, but today I tell all. When I am with other people, my guardian Angel never leaves me; however, when I am with her[14], the angel immediately leaves me (I mean to say that he does not show himself anymore, except to give me some warnings); the same thing happened today: he never left my side for a minute; if I have to speak, to pray, to do something, he lets me know. May Jesus not allow me to be deceived.

This thing so astounds me that it obliged me to ask of him: "How is it that when Mrs. Cecilia is with me, you never stay around?" He answered like this: "No person, other than she, knows how to take my place. Poor girl," he added, "you are so little that you always need a guide! Fear not, for now I shall do it, but obey, you know, because I could easily ... "

I went to confession; I told this to my confessor (I had also written to him about it); so he explained what I did not understand, so now I understand everything.

SATURDAY, AUGUST 11

It's Saturday; I'm going to Holy Communion. What shall I do? Whatever, I shall obey. If only I could obtain a little visit from my Mom.[15] But no, I remember the sin I committed last night. It's true that this morning I confessed myself immediately, but alas, the Blessed Virgin does not forgive so easily, especially with me. She wants me to be perfect.

It's Saturday evening, my God! What punishment! It's the biggest punishment you can give me, depriving me of a visit from Most Holy Mary, and it's precisely around Saturday that I always fall into many omissions.

SUNDAY, AUGUST 12

Sunday has arrived. What indifference, what dryness! Still, I do not want to abandon my usual prayers.

---

[14] Cecilia Giannini.
[15] The Blessed Virgin Mary.

WEDNESDAY, AUGUST 15

FEAST OF THE ASSUMPTION OF MARY INTO HEAVEN

I remained in this state of dryness and the absence of Jesus until today, Wednesday. Since Friday I've heard nothing. My confessor assures me this is a punishment for my sins or to see if I can stay without Jesus, and to stimulate me to love him more. I have been alone throughout, I mean without Jesus. My guardian Angel has not left me for even a second; yet, how many omissions, how many faults even in his presence! My God, have mercy on me! I always went to Communion but Jesus was like He wasn't there anymore. But would Jesus wish to leave me alone even today on such a great holy day? I received communion with much more consolation, but without feeling Jesus. I prayed a lot these days, because I want a grace from Jesus.

Today Mother Maria Teresa should go to Heaven; I hope so. But how will I know? I can't collect myself unless I am in a safe place. Today my guardian Angel will stand guard at my door.

Here I am at 9:15 of this great day. I feel the usual internal collection; I prayed to my guardian Angel to stand guard so that no one should see me; I hid in a room for the nuns.

Oh, not much time passed before collection was followed by rapture. (Whoever reads this should not believe anything, because I could very well be deceived; may Jesus never permit such a thing! I do so for obedience, and I oblige myself to write with great disgust.)

It was around 9:30 and I was reading; all of a sudden I am shaken by a hand resting gently on my left shoulder. I turn in fright; I was afraid and tried to call, but I was held back. I turned and saw a person dressed in white; I recognized it was a woman; I looked and her expression assured me I had nothing to fear: "Gemma," she said after some moments, "do you know me?" I said no, because that was the truth; she responded: "I am Mother Maria Teresa of the Infant Jesus: I thank you so, so much for the great concern you have shown me because soon I shall be able to attain my eternal happiness."

All this happened while I was awake and fully aware of myself.

Then she added: "Continue still, because I still have a few days of suffering." And in so saying she caressed me and then went away.

Her countenance, I must say, inspired much confidence in me. From that hour I redoubled my prayers for her soul, so that soon she should reach her objective; but my prayers are too weak; how I wish that for the souls in Purgatory my prayers should have the strength of the saints'.

From that moment I suffered constantly because until about 11:00pm I could not be alone. I felt inside me a certain sense of collection, a desire to go and pray, but how to do it? I couldn't. How many times I had to insist! Finally I had the longed–for permission, and I went to my Mom; although they were only a few moments, they were precious moments!

Because of my bad behavior, Jesus did not permit the Blessed Virgin to come as She always did, smiling, but instead very sad (and I was the cause). She reproached me a little but cheered up about one thing (that I think here it would be better not to say), and this thing also gave great consolation to Jesus! And in fact it was to reward me for this thing that She came, but as I said, in a serious mood; She said a few words, among them: "Daughter, when I go to Heaven this morning, I shall take your heart with me."

In that moment I felt as if She approached ... removed it from me, took it with Her, in Her hands, and said to me: "Fear nothing, be good; I shall keep your heart forever up there with me, always in my hands." She blessed me hurriedly and in going away She pronounced these words as well: "To Me you have given your heart, but Jesus wants something else as well." "What does he want?" I asked. "Your will," She answered, and vanished.

I found myself on the ground but I know exactly when that happened; it was when She began to approach me and remove my heart.

Although these things frighten me upon first appearance, still at the finish I always end up being in infinite consolations.

THURSDAY, AUGUST 16

Here I am at Thursday. The usual disgust descends upon me; fear of losing my soul comes over me; the number of my sins and their enormity, all open up before me. What agitation! In these moments my guardian Angel suggested in my ear: "But God's mercy is infinite." I calmed down.

Early in the day the pain in my head began; it must have been around 10:00. When I was alone I threw myself on the bed; I suffered some but Jesus was not long in appearing, showing me that He also suffered greatly. I reminded him of the sinners for whom He Himself urged me to offer all my little aches to the Eternal Father on their behalf.

While I was with Jesus and suffering, and He suffered also, a strong desire came upon me, almost impossible to resist. Jesus realized this, and asked me: "What do you want me to do?" And I immediately: "Jesus, have pity, lighten Mother Maria Teresa's torments." And Jesus: "I have already done so. Do you wish anything else?" He asked. That gave me courage and I said: "Jesus, save her, save her." And Jesus answered like this: "On the third day after the Assumption of my Blessed Mother, she will be released from Purgatory and I will take her with me to Heaven."

Those words filled me with a joy such that I do not know how to express it. Jesus said a number of other things; I also asked why after Holy Communion He did not allow me to taste the sweetness of Heaven. He answered promptly: "You are not worthy, oh daughter," but He promised that the next morning he would do it.

How could I pass the time until morning? It's true, only a few hours remained but for me they were years; I didn't close my eyes in sleep; I was consumed, I wanted morning to come immediately: in a word, that night seemed like forever to me, but finally morning has come.

FRIDAY, AUGUST 17

Jesus, as soon as he arrived on my tongue (the cause so often of so many sins), made Himself felt immediately. I was no longer in myself but Jesus was in me; He descended to my breast. (I say breast, because I no longer have a heart; I gave it to Jesus' Mom.) What happy moments I spent with Jesus! How could I return His affections? With what words could I express His love, and for this poor creature? Yet He did deign to come. It's truly impossible, yes, it is impossible not to love Jesus. How many times He asked me if I love Him and if I truly love Him. And do you still doubt it, my Jesus? So, He unites ever more closely with me, talks to me, says He wants me to be perfect, that He too loves me very much and I should reciprocate.

My God, how can I make myself worthy of so many graces? Where I cannot reach, my beloved guardian Angel will take my place. May God never let me deceive myself nor others.

I spent the rest of the day united with Jesus; I suffer a little but no one sees my suffering; only from time to time does some lament come forth but, my God, it is truly involuntary.

Today it took very little, indeed nothing, for me to collect myself: my mind was already with Jesus and I immediately went in spirit as well. How affectionate Jesus showed Himself to be today. But how He suffers! I do what I can to diminish the anguish and I would do more if I had permission. He came near today, lifted the crown from my head, and then I did not see Him replace it as usual on his head; He held it in His hands, all his wounds were open, but they did not drip blood as usual. They were beautiful.

He usually blesses me before leaving, and in fact He lifted his right hand; from that hand I then saw a ray of light shine forth, much stronger than a lamp. He kept his hand raised; I remained fixed in watching it, I could not get enough of Him. Oh if I could make everyone know and see how beautiful is my Jesus. He blessed me with that same hand He had raised, and He left me. After this happened to me, I wanted to know the meaning of the light that shone from his wounds, in particular from his right hand, the one he blessed me with. My guardian Angel said these words to me: "Daughter, on this day Jesus' blessing has showered an abundance of graces upon you."

Now that I am writing this he approached me and said: "I urge you, my daughter, always to obey, and in everything. Reveal everything to your confessor; tell him not to neglect you but to keep you hidden." And then he added: "Tell him that Jesus wants him to have much more concern toward you, that he give you more thought, because otherwise you are too inexperienced."

He repeated these things even after I had written them; he said them many times, when I was awake, and I felt as if I actually saw him and heard him speak. Jesus, may your holy will always be done.

But how I suffer for the obligation to write certain things. The disgust I felt initially, instead of diminishing keeps growing enormously, and I am enduring deathly anguish. How many times today I tried to find and burn all my writings. And then? You maybe, oh my God, You would like me to write also about those hidden things, that You let me know out of your goodness, in order always to keep me low and humble me? If you wish, oh Jesus, I'm ready to do even that: make Your will known. But these writings, of what benefit are they? For your greater glory, oh Jesus, or to make me fall into more and more sin? You wished me to do so, and I did. You think about it. In the wound of your sacred side, oh Jesus, I hide my every word.

SATURDAY – SUNDAY, AUGUST 18 – 19

During Holy Communion this morning Jesus let me know that tonight at midnight Mother Maria Teresa will fly to Heaven. Nothing else for now.

Jesus promised to give me a sign. Midnight has come, nothing yet; now it's 1:00am, still nothing; toward 1:30 it looked to me like the Blessed Virgin would come to give me news, since the hour was approaching.

After a little while in fact I thought I saw that Mother Teresa was coming, dressed as a Passionist, accompanied by her guardian Angel and by Jesus. How she had changed since that day I first saw her. Laughing, she approached me and said she was truly happy and was going to enjoy her Jesus in eternity; she thanked me again and added: "Tell Mother Giuseppa that I am happy and set her at ease." She made a sign several times with her hand to say goodbye and together with Jesus and her guardian angel she flew to Heaven around 2:30am. That night I suffered a lot because I too wanted to go to heaven, but no one thought to take me.

The desire Jesus had nurtured in me for so long finally was satisfied; Mother Teresa is in heaven; but even from heaven she promised to return to see me."

PART IV

AUGUST 20TH TO SEPTEMBER 3RD 1900

MONDAY, AUGUST 20

Yesterday during the day I had to talk with my guardian angel once again; he reproached me above all for my laziness about prayer; he reminded me of many other things: all about the eyes, still, he threatened me severely. Last night in church he reminded me again of what he had said that day, telling me I would have to reckon with Jesus. Finally, before going to bed, as I was asking his blessing, he warned me that today, August 20, Jesus wished me to undergo an assault from the demon, this because for several days I had been negligent in prayer. He warned me that the devil would make every effort to prevent me from praying, especially mentally for all of today, and he would also deprive me of his visit (I mean my guardian angel's), but only for today.

I went to Holy Communion, but who knows in what a state! So distracted —with my mind still on last night – that is, on a bad dream, which I recognized as the work of the devil.

Oh God, the moment of the assault has come; and it was strong, even terrible I would almost say. No sign of the cross, no scapular was enough to halt the most ugly temptation one could imagine; he was so horrifying that I closed my eyes and never opened them again until I was absolutely freed.

My God, if I am without sin, I owe it only to you. You be thanked. What to say in those moments? To look for Jesus and not find him is a greater penance than the temptation itself. What I feel only Jesus knows, who watches secretly and is pleased. At a certain point when it seemed the temptation would take on more force, it came to mind to invoke the holy father of Jesus, and I shouted: "Eternal Father, for the blood of Jesus free me."

I don't know what happened; that good–for–nothing devil gave me such a strong shove that I fell off the bed, causing me to bang my head on the floor with such great force that I felt a sharp pain; I fainted and remained on the ground for a long time before regaining consciousness.

Jesus be thanked, that today also everything turned out in the best way, as He wished. The rest of the day went wonderfully. In the evening, as it happens to me many times, all my grave sins came to mind but with such enormity that I had to make a great effort not to cry out loud: I felt a pain more alive than I had ever undergone before. The number of my sins surpasses by a thousand fold my age and my capacity; but what consoled me is that I endured the greatest pain because of my sins, so that I wished this pain would never be canceled from my mind and never be diminished. My God! to what point my malice has reached!

This evening, to say the truth, I was awaiting Jesus – no way! No one showed up; only my guardian Angel does not cease to watch over me, to instruct me and to give me wise counsel. Many times during the day he reveals himself to me and talks to me. Yesterday he kept me company while I ate but he didn't force me like the others do. After I had eaten, I didn't feel at all well so he brought me a cup of coffee so good that I was healed instantly and then he made me rest a little. Many times I make him ask Jesus for permission to stay with me all night; he goes to ask and then he does not leave me until morning, if Jesus approves.

TUESDAY, AUGUST 21

I may perhaps be wrong, but today I await a little visit from Brother Gabriel and if this is true, I have a lot to talk about with him. Jesus, give light, give light not to me but to Father Germano and to my confessor.

WEDNESDAY, AUGUST 22

Yesterday my guardian Angel informed me that in the course of the day Jesus would come; he[16] yelled at me, called me conceited, but then we made up quickly. I did not think further about Jesus'

---

[16] The Angel.

visit because I did not believe it; but in getting ready for evening prayers I felt in union with Jesus, who instantly reproached me sweetly, saying: "Gemma, don't you want me anymore?" "Oh my God, my God," I answered him, "what do you mean, I don't seek you? I desire you everywhere, I want you, I seek you always, I yearn only for you."

Then right away it came to my mind to ask him: "But Jesus, you came tonight so that means you won't come tomorrow night?" He promised me that He would. But my confessor told me that my conscience would be responsible if I suffered and then did not feel well; if I feel well, I may suffer the usual hour with Jesus; if not, let Jesus come anyway but without making me suffer; I may stay with him and have compassion for him and take part with him in the deathly sadness he suffered in the Garden of Olives. Anyway, I shall obey.

Jesus also spoke to me, without my bringing it up, of the holy soul of Mrs. Giuseppina Imperiali. "Oh how dear she is to Me!" Jesus repeated. "See," He added, "how much she suffers, without a moment of peace. Happiness to her!" He left me with an ineffable sense of consolation, as usual.

For the grace of Jesus and for his infinite mercy, my guardian Angel does not leave me for even a tiny second. Yesterday I saw several angels: mine assisted me continuously and I saw another for another person, and here there certainly is no need to record further all the details; if obedience should require it, I shall be ready, but for now . . . that is enough . . . If necessary, I shall remember.

THURSDAY, AUGUST 23

Alas, evening comes and the usual coldness, the usual repugnance assails me; fatigue would want to win over me, but with a little effort I never want to neglect to do my duty.

Tonight Jesus placed his crown on my head at about 10:00, after I had been collected for a little while. My suffering, which in no way equals Jesus', was very strong: even all my teeth hurt; any movement brought a sharp pain; I thought I could not resist but instead I did, everything went well.

I offered those little penances for sinners and in particular for my poor soul. I begged Him to return soon. When he was about to leave, a contest sprang up between me and Jesus: which of us would be the first to visit (and I went first, I mean to Holy Communion) and together we said and we agreed that I would go to Him and He would come to me. He promised me the assistance of my holy Angel, and He left me.

FRIDAY, AUGUST 24

Later Jesus returned to take back His crown but he came very early, saying I had already done a lot; and since I did not want to, because I did not keep it the usual number of hours, He answered that I was still little, and this is more than enough. I suffered continuously for several hours; Jesus caressed me a lot. At a certain point in our discussion I asked enlightenment for my confessor; on that point my guardian Angel had tattled on Jesus. The morning before he had told me how Father Germano is enlightened about me and how he cares for me. I mentioned this to Jesus without thinking, and Jesus did not know that my guardian Angel had told me this; he made a serious face and told me He did not want my guardian Angel to tattle on him.

While he was talking in this way, instead of being speechless, as happens when Jesus becomes serious or severe, I was taken, on the contrary, with more intimacy toward Him, and I asked: "Jesus, could you not ... " I kept quiet, thinking to make myself understood without speaking further, and Jesus did understand instantly and responded: "Do not be afflicted, my daughter: we will make use of Father Germano soon enough. Do you understand?" He asked. "Yes," I answered. And at the end he repeated these words: "Fear not, because soon we will use him." He raised His hand goodbye and disappeared.

Still later I went to church for the usual blessing but I felt tired; in fact I truly was, but it is not, as I've said many times, true tiredness; it is laziness, a lack of desire to pray. My guardian Angel whispered in my ear that I should pray even while sitting. At first I could not give in but he insisted a second time and so for obedience I remained sitting. For sure I was pleased about this, since I was unable to stay on my knees.

Last night he also made me understand that when Jesus complains about me because I do not do my meditation, He does not mean Thursday and Friday, He means the other days of the week; in fact it's true, because on those two days I never forget. I promised to be more conscientious, and he ordered me to bed, saying I was tired and I had to sleep. I urged him to stay with me but he made no promise, and in fact he did not stay.

"Now then," I said to him, "run to Jesus and plead with him, because tomorrow evening I must go to confession and I need to see him"; and he instantly responded: "And if Brother Gabriel should come?" "That would be the same," I answered. "Either Jesus or Brother Gabriel, one way or another I need a visit; beg Him to concede me this grace, I need it." "Can you tell me?" he asked. "As for you," I responded, "go to Jesus and tell him everything and then return and tell me." He nodded yes.

He had spoken to me a few minutes ago about Brother Gabriel and, as always, even just hearing about him made me happy all over, so I could not refrain from exclaiming: "Brother Gabriel, how long I have been awaiting him, how much I desire him!" 'Just so, because you have such a strong desire, Jesus does not want to satisfy you." Then, laughing, he instructed me that when Jesus came I should not let him know that I had a desire to see Brother Gabriel, in which case Jesus would grant my wish easily.

I realized he was kidding, because I know nothing can be hidden from Jesus.

"Show indifference," he repeated, "and you will see that Jesus will send him more often." "I won't be able to do that," I said. "I'll teach you; you have to talk like this to Jesus: If he comes, fine, if not, it's all the same." And in saying this he laughed heartily.

So I also repeated the phrase but I understood that he was having fun. He ordered me to bed, saying I had to stay alone that night, because if he stayed I would never get to sleep, and he left.

It's true, because when he is there I do not sleep: he teaches me so many things about Heaven and the night passes quickly, very quickly. But last night was not like that: he left me alone, and I slept, although I did awaken several times and instantly he said: "Sleep, otherwise I'm going away for real."

I heard loud thunderclaps, very loud, and I was afraid; so he came and made himself visible; he blessed me once again and I went back to sleep.

SATURDAY, AUGUST 25

During Communion this morning no consolation; I did everything coldly. Let the holy will of my God be done. What will happen today? Jesus is not coming, and I don't even feel Him nearby. I go to bed and I see a guardian Angel approaching, whom I recognized to be mine; but I was overtaken with a bit of fear and an internal disquiet.

So many times fear assails me when I see someone appear but little by little this passes and ends in consolation. Yesterday, instead, my disquiet grew until, if someone touched me, I shook: something that never happens to me when it is truly my dear Angel. In short, I was uncertain about this when he asked me: "When are you going to confession?" "This evening," I answered. "And why? Why do you go so often? Don't you know that your confessor is a swindler?" Then I understood what was happening here and I made the sign of the cross several times; he struck me so severely that I shook. My Angel never speaks to me this way.

The combat lasted in this way for a long while and I promised that in spite of him I would go to confession, and in fact I went. I called Jesus, and my Mom, but what! No one. After a while my real guardian Angel appeared, obliging me to confess every detail and he specified two things to tell my confessor.

Distress and fear of the enemy vanished quickly and I calmed down until it was time to go to confession; I didn't want to go for anything. With effort I went but I was able to say very, very little. But I do want to tell everything, so I will write.

Last night my beloved Mother came, but Her visit was so short; nevertheless it consoled me greatly. I prayed to Her as much as I could on my own behalf, that She take me to Heaven, and I also prayed fervidly for other matters. How She smiled when I repeatedly called her Mom! She came near, caressed me, and left me in the company of my guardian Angel, who remained joyful and cheerful until morning.

SUNDAY, AUGUST 26

In the morning, after I left my room, he also left. I received Holy Communion without knowing anything of Jesus; during the morning I felt such a strong wish to cry that I had to hide myself out of the sight of others so they wouldn't notice. My soul felt uneasy and I did not know what to rely on. My God, how shall I begin to describe it! But it's for the best, because if this notebook of mine should fall into people's hands, they will recognize in me nothing other than a disobedient, bad person.

Yesterday, while eating, I raised my eyes and saw my guardian Angel looking at me with an expression so severe I was frightened; he did not speak. Later, when I went to bed for a moment, my God! He commanded me to look him in the face; I looked and then almost immediately I lowered my gaze, but he insisted and said: "Aren't you ashamed to commit sins in my presence? You certainly feel ashamed after you commit them!" He insisted I look at him; for more than half an hour he made me stay in his presence looking him in the face; he gave me some very stern looks.

I did nothing but cry. I commended myself to my God, to our Mother, to get me out of there, because I could not resist much longer. Every so often he repeated: "I am ashamed of you." I prayed that others would not see him in that state, because then no one would ever come near me; I don't know if others saw him.

I suffered for an entire day, and whenever I lifted my eyes, he always looked at me sternly; I could not collect myself for even a minute. That evening I said my prayers anyway, and he was always there watching me with the same expression; he let me go to bed, but he did bless me; he never abandoned me: he stayed with me for several hours, without speaking and always stern. I never did have the courage to speak a word to him; I only said: "My God, what shame if others should see my angel so angry!"

There was no way I could sleep last night; I was awake until after 2:00; I know, because I heard the clock strike. I stayed in bed, not moving, my mind turned to God but without praying. Finally, after the clock struck 3: 00, I saw my guardian Angel approaching; he placed his hand on my forehead and said these words: "Sleep, bad girl" I saw him no more.

MONDAY, AUGUST 27

This morning I received Holy Communion: I hardly had the courage to receive it. Jesus seemed to let me know a little about why my guardian Angel was acting this way: I had made my last confession badly. Unfortunately, this was true.

TUESDAY, AUGUST 28

My guardian Angel remained very stern until this morning, after I revealed everything to my confessor. Upon my exiting from the confessional, he looked at me happily, with an air of kindness: I returned from death to life. Later he spoke to me on his own (I did not have the courage to question him) he asked me how I was, because I was not feeling well the night before. I answered that only he could cure me;[17] he came near, caressed me again and again, and said I should be good.

Repeatedly I asked him if he loved me as much as before and if he loved me despite everything; he answered in this way: "Today I am not ashamed of you, yesterday I was." I asked many times for forgiveness and he indicated that I was forgiven for every past action. Finally, I sent him to Jesus for three things: (1) If He was happy with me now? (2) If He had forgiven everything? (3) That He should rid me of this shame so that I could be obedient to my confessor.

He went away instantly and returned very late; he said Jesus was very happy; that He has forgiven me, but for the last time; as to the shame, he said Jesus responded with these exact words:

---

[17] Gemma did not feel well because her Angel was angry at her due to the poor Confession she had previously made, hence she was seeking his forgiveness.

"Tell her to obey perfectly." Later, then, I went to bed and after a little while I felt some remorse. I was thinking, it's true, on the subject of a meditation on the Passion, but in bed. My guardian Angel asked what I was thinking. "About the Passion," I answered, "what will Jesus say about me, who leads such an easy life, praying little, and in bed; in short, all my time in prayer I spend in bed?" Unfortunately, all this is true. He answered by asking what I thought. "It is laziness," I responded. But I promised that from that evening on I would never again pray in bed; except for the day that I was supposed to, out of obedience. Last evening and for the whole night he never left me, but with an agreement: I must be quiet and sleep. I did it.

WEDNESDAY, AUGUST 29

Today there's one thing I shall do: I want to write a little note to Brother Gabriel; then I'll give it to my guardian Angel and await a reply. And we're going to do this without Jesus knowing; he himself said we will not tell Jesus anything.

And I did it: I wrote a very long letter; I spoke of all my experiences without leaving out anything; then I advised my guardian Angel that it was ready, and if he wanted to ... This evening, Wednesday, I placed it under my pillow, and this morning when I got up I didn't think about checking because I had better things in mind: I was going to Jesus.[18]

THURSDAY, AUGUST 30

As soon as I returned I looked, and how odd! The letter wasn't there anymore. I say odd because I heard from others that this is a strange happening; but to me it doesn't seem so. My guardian angel then asked me if I needed an answer. I laughed. "What else," I told him, "of course I need one." "All right," he said, "but until Saturday you can't have one." Patience, until Saturday then.

In the meantime, here I am at Thursday evening. Oh God! All my sins are paraded before me. What an enormity! Yes, all of

---

[18] To Mass.

you should know; my life until now has been a continuous series of sins. Always I see their great quantity, and the malicious intent with which I committed them, especially when Thursday evening approaches; they parade before me in a manner so frightening that I become ashamed and unbearable even to myself. So, especially that evening, I make resolutions and repent continuously; but then I keep none of them and return to my usual ways. A little strength, a little courage comes to me when I feel Jesus at the hour when he places the crown of thorns on me and makes me suffer until Friday evening, because this I offer for sinful souls, especially my own.

This is how things went yesterday evening, Thursday; I thought Jesus would do like usual that evening: He placed the crown of thorns on my head, the cause of so much pain for my beloved Jesus, and left it there for several hours. It made me suffer a little but when I say suffering I mean taking pleasure. It is a pleasure, that suffering. How He was afflicted! And the cause: for the many sins committed, and the many ungrateful souls whom He assists, only to receive in return exactly the opposite. Of this ingratitude how much I feel guilty myself! For sure, Jesus must have spoken of me.

My guardian Angel warned me that the hour allowed to me for obedience had ended; what to do? Jesus would have stayed longer, but He saw clearly the embarrassing situation I found myself in. I reminded myself about obedience, and for obedience I should have sent Jesus away, because the hour was up. "Come on," said Jesus, "give me a sign now that you will always obey." So I exclaimed: "Jesus, you can go away because now I don't want you anymore." And Jesus smiled as He blessed me, along with all the members of the Sacra Collegio, and He commended me to my guardian Angel, and left me so happy that I cannot express myself.

As usual, that night I cannot sleep because I am united with Jesus, united more closely than usual, and also because I think my head aches a bit; I kept vigil together with my beloved Angel.

FRIDAY, AUGUST 31

In the morning I ran to receive Holy Communion, but I could not say anything; I just stayed in silence; the pain in my head impeded me. My God, how much I lack in this! Jesus held back nothing on my behalf while I instead, in order not to suffer, avoid making even the slightest movement if I can. What would you say, my Jesus, about this laziness and ill will?

All morning I did nothing but rest. Day came and effortlessly I flew to Jesus; He lifted the thorns and asked if I had suffered much. "Oh, my Jesus," I exclaimed, "the suffering begins now because you go away. Yesterday and today, I took much pleasure because I felt close to You; but from now on, until You return, it will truly be constant suffering for me." I implored him "Come, my Jesus, come more often: I will be good, I will always obey everyone. Make me happy, Jesus." I suffered as I spoke this way because little by little Jesus was leaving me.

Finally after a short while He left me alone, once again in the usual state of abandonment. Toward evening I went to confession and the confessor, believing I was not feeling well, because I had been suffering some, ordered me to go to bed as soon as I entered my room, and he ordered me to sleep, without speaking with my guardian Angel (because sometimes we would talk for hours on end), and that I should sleep.

I went to bed but I could not fall asleep out of the curiosity I had; I wanted to ask my guardian Angel so many things, and I waited for him to speak on his own, but no way! All he told me was to go to sleep, several times. Finally I fell asleep.

SATURDAY, SEPTEMBER 1

This morning on his own he awakened me early and said that today I would have an answer. "How?" I asked. "You will see," he said, laughing.

For all of today I stayed without any temptations; toward evening one suddenly came over me, in the ugliest manner. But here I don't think it would be good to tell, because it's too ...

Who would have imagined that my beloved Mother would come to see me? I wasn't even thinking about it because I believed my bad conduct wouldn't allow it; but She took pity on me and in a short time I felt collected; following this collection, as so often happened, my head took off. I found myself (I thought) with Our Lady of Sorrows. What happiness in those moments. How dear to pronounce the name Mom! What sweetness I felt in my heart in those moments! Let whoever is able to, explain it. It seemed to me, after a few minutes of commotion, that She took me in her lap and made me rest my head on Her shoulder, keeping me there a while. My heart in that moment was filled with happiness and contentment; I could desire nothing more. "Do you love no one but Me?" She asked from time to time. "Oh no," I answered, "I love someone else even more than You."

"And who is that?" She asked, pretending not to know. "It's a person who is most dear to me, more than anything else; I love Him so much I would give up my life this very instant; because of Him I no longer care about my body." "But tell me who He is," She asked impatiently. "If You had come the evening before last, You would have seen Him staying with me. But You see, He comes to me very rarely while I go to him every day, and I would go even more often if I could. But do you know, dear Mother" I said, "why He does this? Because He wants to see whether at so great a distance I might become capable of not loving Him anymore; instead, the further away He is, the more I feel drawn to him." She repeated: "Tell me who He is." "No, I won't tell you," I responded. "You should see, dear Mom, how his beauty resembles yours, your hair is the same color as His." And it seemed my Mom was caressing me as She said, "But, My daughter, who are you talking about?" And I exclaimed loudly: "Don't you understand me? I'm talking about Jesus. About Jesus," I repeated even more loudly. She looked at me, smiling, and she hugged me tightly to her:

"Go ahead and love Him, love Him very much, but love only Him." "Don't be afraid," I said, "no one in the world shall taste my affections, only Jesus."

She hugged me again and it seemed like She kissed me on the forehead; I awoke and found myself on the floor, with the crucifix nearby.

Whoever reads these things, I repeat again, should not believe, because they are all my imagination; nevertheless I agree to describe everything, because I am bound by obedience, otherwise I would do differently. I believed that from day to day the repugnance I experience in writing certain things would finally cease, but instead it always increases: it is a punishment such that I cannot withstand, I almost die from it.

SUNDAY, SEPTEMBER 2

Tonight I slept with my guardian Angel by my side; upon awakening I saw him next to me; he asked me where I was going. "To Jesus," I answered.

The rest of the day went very well. But my God, toward evening what happened! My guardian Angel got serious and stern; I could not figure out the reason, but he, from whom nothing can be hidden, in a stern tone (at the moment when I started to recite my usual prayers) asked me what I was doing. "I am praying." "Who are you waiting for?" (becoming yet more serious). Without thinking, I said: "Brother Gabriel." Upon hearing me pronounce those words he started to yell at me, saying I was waiting in vain, just as I could wait in vain for the response[19] because ...

And here I remember two sins I had committed during the day. My God, what sternness! He pronounced these words more than once: "I am ashamed of you. I will end up by not coming to you anymore, and maybe ... who knows if even tomorrow." And he left me in that state. He made me cry so much. I want to ask forgiveness but when he is that angry, there is no way he wants to forgive.

---

[19] To my letter.

MONDAY, SEPTEMBER 3

I did not see him again that night, nor this morning; today he told me to adore Jesus, who was alone, and then he disappeared again.

This evening it was much better than the evening before; I asked him many times for forgiveness and he seemed willing to forgive me. Tonight he stayed with me constantly: he repeated that I should be good and not give further disgust to our Jesus, and when I am in his presence, I should try to be better..

THE END

.INRI PUBLISHERS, COPYRIGHT 2012

Printed in Great Britain
by Amazon.co.uk, Ltd.,
Marston Gate.